Printed in the United States of America

A Red Dock Publishing book,
released by
Pisgah Press, LLC
PO Box 9663
Asheville, NC 28815-0663

Book layout and design by A.D. Reed
www.pisgahpress.com

Cover design by Anna Fong Designs

Photo acknowledgments on p. 90-91.

Library of Congress Cataloging-in-Publication Data
Stewart, Jon/CLASS E 151-909 E813-816
U.S. History Truman Era

ISBN: 978-1-942016-83-0

First Print Edition November 2023

MAGDALENA

The Second Roswell Crash

JON STEWART

Red Dock Publishing
released by
Pisgah Press, LLC

Acknowledgements

Iextend my heartfelt gratitude to those who have shown remarkable patience, courtesy, and kindness by sharing their knowledge and collaboration on this extraordinary journey. A profound thank you goes to the following individuals and teams:

Donald Schmitt, affectionately known as "Uncle Don"

Anna Fong, my art design guru

Rev. Michael J. Carter

Investigator Chris Jackson

My agent, Shawn West

My editor, Andy Reed

The entire UFO Hunters Team, whose enthusiasm reignited my interest in the Magdalena crash.

I am immensely thankful to the incredible group of internet supporters who have reached out through calls, letters, texts, and emails, offering their well wishes. Your kind words hold immeasurable significance to me.

Thank you to my sister Jill, "The Godmudder," for reminding me over the past five years that I'm not crazy.

I also acknowledge veteran journalist William P. Barrett for his admirable investigative prowess. William's commitment to old-school journalistic principles is admirable, and I've strived to follow in his footsteps—diligently working the phones, chasing leads and witnesses, and personally knocking on doors. It brings to mind the sage advice I received from famed Chicago Police Sergeant William Giaconetti at the outset of my UFO research:

"You can't unravel a mystery, solve a murder, or find a missing person, by remaining glued to a desk and your computer."

My gratitude also goes to Dr. Steven Greer, whose unwavering acceptance and graciousness have overwhelmed me. Dr. Greer, you are a true gentleman.

I also extend my heartfelt appreciation to former USAF Special Agent Richard M. Doty, whose guidance has lifted the veil on the path to disclosure and, like a true friend, illuminated my way forward. I will be eternally grateful for your invaluable contributions to both my professional and personal life.

And finally, to my present and future grandchildren and great-grandchildren, never stop believing in yourself—and question everything.

Jon Stewart

November 28, 2023

Introduction

For over two decades, I have traversed the winding roads of UFO research, delving into the mysteries that hover above our skies. It's a pursuit that has led me through countless reports, witness testimonies, and intriguing incidents. Yet amidst the wealth of stories, one enigma stood out—the elusive, often whispered, tale of the Second Roswell Crash.

The Roswell incident of 1947 has long captivated the imaginations of those curious about the most famous UFO event in history. While the first crash in Roswell (Corona), New Mexico, has been dissected, dissected again, and analyzed from every angle imaginable, the shadows of another incident, one less well-known but no less compelling, lurked in the background.

As a UFO researcher, I have been compelled to explore this intriguing chapter of UFO lore, driven by the realization that no comprehensive account existed that compiled the scattered stories of the forgotten second Roswell Crash witnesses. My pursuit led me through dusty archives, the relentless embrace of the desert's scorching sun, abandoned, hollowed-out buildings, and to the "electronic doorsteps" of the few left who still have accounts to relate.

UFO research, at times, can be tedious and repetitive, with an unending supply of stories describing arid sand, scattered metallic pieces and a plethora of data. In a community where anecdotes and stories are the currency, we are acutely aware of the burden we bear—to sift through the anecdotal, the speculative, and the truly extraordinary. Outlandish tales may abound, but for over eighty years, such stories have been the very lifeblood of the UFO community—a weighty cross we willingly carry as we embark on this voyage into the heart of the unknown.

Yet, as I approached the narrative of this book, I was determined to give these second crash witnesses their proper due, to breathe life into their accounts, and to engage the reader with vibrant and captivating prose.

In the pages that follow, we make no attempt to sway the argument one way or the other. Our mission is clear—to compile, relate, and disseminate the accounts of the second Roswell crash. We invite you to join us on this journey, to suspend your disbelief, and to explore the enigmatic events that have remained shrouded in mystery for far too long. Magdalena awaits, a hidden chapter in the annals of UFO history, and we invite you to unravel its secrets alongside us.

This book is in honor of those who have long since departed this world, the second Roswell crash "Flag Bearers" as I respectfully call them. May their voices, tales and accounts now echo through the corridors of history.

"Even the lightning strikes silently, the thunder that you hear is the proclamation of its victory."

—Nabaneet Mandal

Jon Stewart

Dedication

This book is dedicated to my beloved wife, Jojo, and our precious children, Alexandra and Allison, who have gracefully weathered the whirlwind of living with an E.T./Alien researcher. Thank you for enduring, without a revolt, the past five years of the Stewart UFO "roller coaster."

MAGDALENA

The
Second
Roswell
Crash

Table of Contents

Chapter 1

Ominous Echoes

Late June 1947—Roswell New Mexico

In the expansive landscape of the New Mexico desert, a group of US Air Force personnel congregated at a corner of the Roswell Army Air Field in June of 1947. Among them was Tom Carey, a young and dedicated airman. Against the backdrop of post-war America, where the world was grappling with the aftermath of conflict, a curious incident unfolded.

On a warm June day, as the sun cast long shadows, Tom and his fellow airmen found themselves staring at the sky. Suspended before their eyes were three peculiar objects, motionless and gleaming in the sunlight. Trained to assess and comprehend, the airmen were confused by the inexplicable scene. However, this event was not isolated. Reports emerged from the townspeople of Roswell, detailing similar sightings of unfamiliar aircraft. The ripples of intrigue spread through the community, weaving together the experiences of military personnel and civilians alike, and setting the stage for a mystery that would intrigue generations to come.

Later that night, nestled within a remote ranch near the San Augustin Plains, a solitary observer emerged from a weathered barn. His gaze was drawn upward, where the titanic thunderheads clashed, sending electrifying bolts of lightning across the horizon. Within this grand spectacle, the rancher's attention was snared by a profound crash towards the Luera Mountains, resounding from the heart of the storm. The very ground seemed to tremble beneath his feet, a tangible testament to the extraordinary event transpiring above. It was a sound that transcended the natural order, a roar that echoed through the landscape and the witness's thoughts alike.

Simultaneously, miles away, outside the tranquil town of Magdalena, a resident stood on a porch, captivated by the vibrant sky dance of the lightning bolts blossoming across the eastern horizon. Yet her gaze was torn from the display by a deep and resonant thud emanating from the vicinity of Horse Peak. This imposing natural monument, silhouetted against the stormy skies, seemed to resonate with the mysterious energy of the event.

The thud's echoes lingered, leaving an eerie silence in its wake. She felt a tingle of anticipation, a recognition that something beyond the ordinary had unfolded. Pre-Fourth of July fireworks and claps of thunder continued their exuberant display, almost in a duel over New Mexico's attention, but the Magdalen resident remained fixated on the mysteries woven into the fabric of the night.

In Corona, 70 miles north of Roswell, an unassuming rancher named W.W. "Mac" Brazel marveled at the storm's intensity. As he moved indoors he made a mental note to inspect his ranch in the coming days for any damage the ferocious storm might have left in its wake.

Some days later, on the evening of July 4th, 1947, another massive thunderstorm enveloped the expansive skies above the Pacific Northwest. While the distant fireworks punctuated Independence Day celebrations across the nation, a different kind of spectacle was about to transpire, hidden within the veils of this tumultuous weather.

That night, United Airlines Flight 105, under the command of Captain Emil Smith, soared through the electrified atmosphere with its three-member crew. Beyond the cockpit windows, the sprawling landscape was intermittently illuminated by flashes of lightning that cast eerie shadows on the landscape. Amid these celestial theatrics, an astounding phenomenon emerged—an array of unidentified flying objects.

Multiple disc-like forms, reflecting the chaotic dance of lightning, suddenly darted across the tempestuous heavens. The crew, captivated by this surreal sight, exchanged incredulous glances. The discs' flight defied all conventional understanding, moving with an agility that far outpaced the capabilities of earthly aircraft.

Questions raced through the crew's minds as they attempted to decipher this extraordinary display. What civilization could harness such technology, transcending the known limits of aviation? The enigma lingered momentarily before the multiple discs vanished as abruptly as they had appeared, leaving an indelible mark on the crew's consciousness.

In those fleeting moments, the lives of Captain Smith, like those of the other observers days earlier, became linked by their shared encounter with the unexplainable. An unveiled enigma loomed large, poised to challenge humanity's understanding of its place within the cosmos. Thus began the odyssey of the second Roswell crash—a tale that would echo through time, resonating with questions and curiosities, shrouded in the allure of the extraterrestrial.

NEW MEXICO

Santa Fe

Albuquerque

Vaughn

"Debris Field"
(Approx. 75 mi.
NW of Roswell)

Clovis

Socorro

San Agustin
Plains

"Crash Site" 1
(North of Roswell;
exact location
unknown)

"Crash Site" 2
(Approx. 175 mi.
NW of Roswell)

Sacramento Mountains

San Andres Mountains

White
Sands
Proving
Ground

Roswell

Walker AFB
(formerly Roswell AAF)

Holloman AFB

Alamogordo

Artesia

Jornada Test Range

San Agustin Pass

Las Cruces

Rio Grande

Pecos

El Paso

| Crash Site 2 Magdalena, NM shown above | Crash Site 1 near Clovis, NM shown above |

There are things known and there are things unknown, and in
between are the doors of perception.

—Aldous Huxley

Chapter 2

A Scattered Enigma

In the aftermath of the tempestuous thunderstorm that had
unleashed its fury upon the New Mexican expanse on July
4, 1947, Mac Brazel stumbled upon a tableau of intrigue that
would rewrite the history of the region, as well as the course of
human understanding.

As dawn broke on the morning of July 5th, Brazel embarked
on an exploration of his remote ranch in Chaves County. The
landscape, now bathed in the gentle glow of morning light, bore
the traces of the storm that had raged just hours before. Amid the
familiar terrain, Mac's eyes were drawn to an unusual scattering
of debris—shimmering, metallic fragments that seemed utterly
out of place.

Intrigued and perplexed, Mac Brazel knelt to inspect the
strange wreckage. The material was unlike any he had ever
encountered—a fusion of strange substances, woven together
in configurations that defied conventional engineering.
Hieroglyphic-like symbols adorned some of the pieces, hinting
at a level of sophistication beyond earthly origins.

A nagging sense of unease settled within Brazel as he
contemplated the unearthly fragments before him. Recognizing
the significance of his discovery, he resolved to share his findings
with the world. On that same Saturday, July 5, he drove to Corona,

New Mexico, to show patrons at a local bar the perplexing debris he had gathered and brought with him.

News of Mac Brazel's discovery spread quickly, reaching the ears of Sheriff George Wilcox. Recognizing the potential implications, he swiftly contacted the Roswell Army Airfield to apprise them of the unusual situation. The matter was subsequently placed under the purview of Major Jesse Marcel and Captain Sheridan Cavitt, setting in motion a chain of events that would forever be etched in the annals of history.

Major Marcel and Captain Cavitt embarked on the journey to the ranch to assess the situation firsthand. Upon arriving at the scene of the apparent crash, they were met with a tableau that defied easy explanation—the surreal sight of otherworldly debris strewn across the arid landscape. It was clear that this was no ordinary occurrence; the materials possessed a peculiar sheen and construction that stood in stark contrast to anything of terrestrial origin.

The subsequent investigation would propel these military officials into the heart of a labyrinthine enigma, a puzzle that would challenge the boundaries of their expertise and reshape the course of human understanding. The wreckage recovered by Mac Brazel held the potential to rewrite the rules of reality itself—a gateway into realms unknown and an unveiling of truths that lay hidden beneath the veneer of everyday life.

The narrative had shifted from the hands of the rancher to the military officers who were thrust into the heart of an extraterrestrial mystery. From Mac Brazel's chance encounter with the unknown to the enigmatic debris field that lay before him, the events of July 5th set the stage for an unfolding saga that would captivate the imagination of generations to come.

We do not remember days, we remember moments.

—Cesare Pavese

Chapter 3

The Morning Reverie

Accompanying Major Marcel and Captain Cavitt on this expedition was Brazel, who had unwittingly stumbled upon the otherworldly debris. As their vehicle navigated the uneven trails, thoughts raced through Jesse Marcel's mind. The material he had seen defied logical explanation. Its intricate patterns and inexplicable composition challenged his understanding of the laws of science and engineering.

As they approached the wreckage, and following their initial assessment of the massive, fan-shaped debris field, Major Marcel and Captain Cavitt embarked on a journey that would lead them deeper into the heart of an unfathomable mystery. Their destination: to make sense of the site where the scattered remnants of the unknown wreckage lay, a puzzle waiting to be deciphered.

Finally arriving at the site, the group was greeted by the surreal tableau of the debris field, bathed in the soft light of the setting sun. Shimmering in the fading light, the fragments seemed to whisper tales of an existence beyond human understanding. Jesse Marcel, Mac Brazel, and Sheridan Cavitt knelt to examine the pieces, their fingers tracing the strange symbols etched into their surfaces.

As night fell, casting an inky shroud over the landscape, the rancher's eyes glittered with a mix of wonder and apprehension. He had uncovered a secret that extended far beyond the boundaries of his remote ranch. The military presence and the peculiar material left him with a sense of unease, an awareness that his life was now entwined with forces beyond his comprehension.

In the quiet hours of the night, a thought took root in Jesse Marcel's mind—an impulse to share his discovery with those closest to him, to validate the reality of the unearthly materials that had consumed his thoughts. Metal, as thin as foil, that molds itself back into its original shape; strange symbols on I-shaped beams . . . Marcel was totally stupefied about the foreign objects that now lay in a box on the back seat of his vehicle. Not a box of bric-a-brac or rummage sale items, but rather a box full of what were possibly the most important historical items in human history.

In the wee hours of the morning, the Marcel residence was illuminated by a soft light. Jesse's wife and son stirred from their slumber. As they entered the kitchen, they were met with a sight that defied all expectations. For here Jesse had brought home the mysterious debris, each piece bathed in the ethereal glow of soft lamplight.

Jesse Marcel's eyes sparkled with a mixture of excitement and trepidation as he gazed at his family. He had brought them into a world that defied their understanding, and in doing so, he sought to bridge the gap between his personal reality and the reality of the otherworldly materials.

For a moment, the Marcell family stood united before the enigmatic scene, grappling with its implications. The kitchen transformed into a sanctum of wonder, a space where the barriers between the known and the unknown seemed to blur.

As the night ebbed away, so did the hours of slumber. When morning light seeped through the windows, it illuminated an empty kitchen—the box of debris was gone, along with its custodian, Jesse Marcel.

Two days would pass before Jesse Marcel reappeared, his absence shrouded in mystery. In those intervening hours, the enigma of the wreckage had been suspended between time and consciousness, a testament to the pull of the inexplicable and the yearning to bridge the gap between human understanding and the cosmic unknown.

In this unfolding saga, Major Jesse Marcel's personal encounter with the unearthly materials took center stage. His midnight revelation to his family and subsequent absence encapsulated the very essence of the mystery, its ability to captivate and confound, to blur the boundaries between reality and perception. As days turned into nights and the mysteries deepened, the trajectory of this narrative remained as unpredictable as the universe itself, with W.W. "Mac" Brazel's silent presence serving as a reminder of the inexplicable journey that had just begun.

There is no greater agony than carrying the burden of an untold story.

—Kanika Dhillon

Chapter 4

A Whisper in the Skies

On the morning of July 8, 1947, the sands of history shifted once more as Major Jesse Marcel carried with him the weight of an extraordinary secret. Cradling the strange debris in his arms, he navigated the corridors of the Roswell Army Air Field toward the office of Colonel William Blanchard, the commander of the 509th Bomb Group.

As he entered the office, Major Marcel's heart raced with a mix of anticipation and trepidation. The office was an island of order in the chaos of this unfolding saga. Colonel Blanchard, his countenance a mixture of curiosity and seriousness, glanced up from his desk.

In the muted light of the room, the debris—its metallic surfaces shimmering faintly—occupied the space between them. Major Marcel's account spilled forth, recounting the journey from discovery to revelation, laying bare the inexplicable, alien nature of the materials before them.

Colonel Blanchard listened intently, his thoughts a whirlwind of realization and consideration. The implications of this discovery extended far beyond the confines of the Roswell Army Airfield. It was a puzzle that demanded immediate attention and assessment at higher echelons.

Following their conversation, Colonel Blanchard swiftly

communicated the gravity of the situation to General Roger Ramey, stationed at Fort Worth Army Airfield. The chain of command buzzed with activity, orders were disseminated, and preparations set in motion for the transfer of the debris.

Within hours, some debris was carefully loaded onto an aircraft bound for Fort Worth Army Airfield. The skies, once witnesses to the boundless expanse of the unknown, now bore witness to a secret journey—one that held the potential to reshape the fabric of human understanding.

By the end of the day, the cloak of secrecy was gradually lifted. Officer Walter Haut, in a historic move, issued a press release that reverberated around the world. The military had indeed recovered a "flying disc" from the Roswell region, a revelation that ignited a frenzy of speculation and curiosity.

As the press release circulated, a crew of dedicated individuals worked diligently, loading the mysterious debris and bodies onto the aircraft that would transport it to Wright Field. Among these individuals was flight engineer Robert Porter, a man poised to become a participant in an unforgettable moment in history.

An alleged photo of a military convoy going thru Roswell July 8, 1947 with an apparently egg-shaped craft under a tarp.

As the plane's cargo hold was loaded, Robert Porter's attention was drawn to an offhand remark, a statement that sent a shiver down his spine: "A flying saucer is in our cargo hold." The words hung in the air like a whisper from the cosmos, a confirmation of the extraordinary nature of their cargo and the mission they were embarking upon.

The narrative in 1947 suddenly pivoted from the initial encounter with the debris to the moment when its reality was made known to a wider world. The corridors of power shifted also, decisions were made, and actions set in motion, all against the backdrop of the unknown that hovered like a specter over every step taken. As the craft, bodies and the remaining debris made its way toward the U.S. Government's Foreign Material Division in Ohio, its journey echoed the journey of humanity itself—into the uncharted territories of the inexplicable, the unfathomable, and the extraordinary.

A lie can run round the world before the truth has got its boots on.

—Charles Spurgeon (also attributed to Mark Twain)

Chapter 5

Rumors and Conjecture

As the enigmatic debris, mangled craft and alien bodies hurtled through the skies en route to Wright Field, questions began to gather like storm clouds in the minds of those privy to this unfolding mystery. Among the foremost queries that lingered in the collective consciousness was a fundamental one: How had this unidentified flying object, this purported flying saucer, met its ignominious end on Earth?

Speculation branched like lightning across the night sky. Some voices wondered if the severe thunderstorm that had raged on the night of July 4th held the key. Was it possible that the intricate interplay of wind, rain, and electric discharge had somehow caused the UFO's demise? Could the brute force of nature, unchecked and unanticipated, have disrupted the delicate equilibrium of this otherworldly craft, propelling it toward its eventual crash? Was it the Russians or some deep, secretive, U.S. Government program known only to a select few?

Others posited an alternative hypothesis—one tinged with an air of conspiracy and intrigue. Could it be that this so-called UFO was, in fact, a covert experiment—a prototype of a new type of weapon being developed by the government? Could a lethal combination of electromagnetic interference, perhaps intended as a weapon, have inadvertently brought the craft down?

This very notion sparked further lines of inquiry. If indeed the government was testing a radical new technology, then why the element of surprise when the debris field was discovered? The Roswell Army Airfield, as a key outpost of military intelligence, was not given to being caught unawares. Could it be that the authorities themselves were taken aback by the catastrophic outcome, leading to the scramble to cover up the incident?

Theories swirled and intersected, each thread a possibility that danced on the precipice of understanding. The answers, however, remained tantalizingly beyond reach. The journey of the debris to Fort Worth only underscored the enigma, casting a shadow that deepened the uncertainty surrounding the origins, motivations, and eventual fate of the unidentified craft.

In the corridors of power, where decisions were being made that would reverberate through history, these questions undoubtedly loomed. Major Jesse Marcel, Colonel William Blanchard, and those privy to the unfolding saga found themselves ensnared by the paradox of knowledge and ignorance, their actions guided by fragments of truth cloaked in shadows of uncertainty.

As whispers of the Roswell UFO incident swirled through the corridors of secrecy, the wreckage—a tantalizing mystery in its own right—embarked on a clandestine journey. From Roswell Army Airfield, it found its way first to Fort Worth, and later, was flown to the enigmatic confines of Wright Field (now Wright-Pateterson Air Force Base). A parallel narrative was meticulously woven, one that sought to cloak the truth in a veil of deception. Through the hands of official statements and press releases, a tale emerged that was designed to deflect the curious gaze of the world.

Yet the shadows of secrets cast long silhouettes, and beyond the well-orchestrated masquerade lay an untouched secret—a second crash site, nestled in the embrace of the Magdalena landscape. Under the unforgiving sun, it remained undiscovered for a span of two years, biding its time as if in silent anticipation of its eventual unveiling, an emblem of a narrative poised between truth and subterfuge.

In the wake of the mounting speculation and intrigue surrounding the Roswell incidents, a new cover story emerged from the Roswell Army Air Field, attempting to douse the flames of curiosity with a seemingly innocuous explanation. According to this narrative, the unidentified debris scattered across the landscape was the subject of this new "official" tale: it was nothing but a weather balloon—a seemingly ordinary object that had assumed an extraordinary role in history. This story, carefully crafted and disseminated, aimed to steer the public's imagination away from the extraordinary and back toward the mundane. Yet, even as this weather balloon narrative took hold, it failed to quell the persistent whispers of a deeper truth, casting a shadow of doubt upon official explanations, and fueling the unrelenting pursuit of what truly transpired during those enigmatic days in Roswell.

A photo op was taken in a room at the Roswell base where Maj. Marcell and Gen. Ramey posed uncomfortably in front of what looked like an aluminum-foil kite made with string and wood. That day, the U.S. Army officially called into question Maj. Marcell's judgment, making a mockery of the preceding day's event. Like a Greek tragedy the most important event in human history is covered up with a laughable prop that tarnished reputations but was adequate—barely—to redirect the public's attention to other news closer to home. Alas, Roswell fades from the public consciousness.

The Roswell Crash Event went from the physical journey of debris to the realm of conjecture and speculation. As humanity grappled with the mystery of how an unidentified flying object had crashed to Earth, myriad possibilities painted a portrait of uncertainty. Theories ranged from natural calamities to clandestine government activities, each layer of hypothesis a testament to the profound and enduring enigma that had captivated the collective imagination.

History has a way of fading memories, but the truth, when rediscovered, has the power to shine brightly once more.

—Author unknown

Chapter 6

What Is Old Becomes New

In the early 1970s, the mystery of the Roswell incident had largely faded into the background, obscured by the passage of time and overshadowed by the tumultuous events of the Cold War. It was in this atmosphere of secrecy and skepticism that physicist Stanton Friedman embarked on a journey that would ultimately breathe new life into the Roswell enigma.

Stanton Friedman, a dedicated physicist with a passion for investigating unexplained phenomena, first encountered the Roswell incident in 1978 during a speaking engagement in Baton Rouge, Louisiana. A casual conversation after his lecture led him down a path that would consume his life and shape his life's work.

At the time, many believed that the Roswell incident, which had occurred in July 1947, involved the crash of a "weather balloon." The U.S. military had officially explained the debris as such, but rumors and conspiracy theories persisted, suggesting

Nuclear physicist and UFOlogist Stanton Friedman

a far more extraordinary event had taken place. For decades, the incident had remained shrouded in mystery, but Friedman was determined to get to the truth.

Friedman's journey began with tireless research and countless interviews with witnesses, many of whom had never before shared their stories. He uncovered a trove of compelling evidence that contradicted the official explanation. Witness testimonies, military documents, and photographs pointed to a different reality—a reality that challenged the narrative the U.S. government had crafted.

One of the key breakthroughs came when Friedman interviewed Jesse Marcel, a central figure in the original Roswell incident. Marcel revealed that the debris he had examined at the crash site was unlike any weather balloon material he had seen. Instead, it had unusual properties, including a metallic, memory-like material that could not be easily explained. Marcel's account was instrumental in challenging the government's weather balloon explanation.

Friedman's tireless efforts to uncover the truth sparked a renewed interest in the Roswell incident. He traveled the country, speaking at conferences, presenting his findings, and urging the public to question the official narrative. His expertise as a nuclear physicist lent credibility to his research, and his unwavering dedication inspired others to take a closer look at the mystery.

As the 1970s drew to a close, Stanton Friedman had successfully reignited the public's fascination with Roswell. His work had become a cornerstone of UFO research, and his dedication had breathed new life into the investigation. The Roswell incident was no longer a forgotten footnote in history; it had become a symbol of the enduring quest for the truth in the face of official secrecy.

Stanton Friedman's role in reviving the Roswell incident's public interest was a pivotal moment in the ongoing search for answers about what truly happened that fateful summer in 1947. His relentless pursuit of the truth would continue to influence generations of researchers and enthusiasts, ensuring that the Roswell enigma would remain a mystery worth unraveling for years to come.

If you tell the truth, you won't have to remember anything.

—Mark Twain

Chapter 7

The Cause of the Crash— Differing Accounts

As the world grappled for decades with the mystery of the Roswell crash, a new chapter unfolded—some that introduced two distinct voices into the already cacophonous chorus of speculation. Richard M. Doty, a former special agent with the Air Force Office of Special Investigations, and Dr. Steven Greer of the Disclosure Project, emerged as figures with differing accounts, each offering a unique perspective on the events surrounding the enigmatic incident. We will share their testimony before we look at other accounts of what happened in the New Mexico desert back in 1947.

Richard M. Doty's presence was marked by his direct briefing of the military's investigative efforts. With a measured demeanor, he corrected those who mistakenly referred to the crash site as Roswell, emphasizing that the debris field was

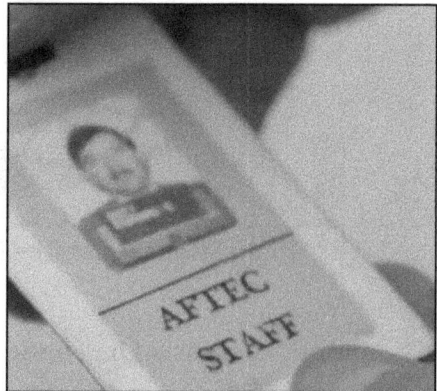

Richard M. Doty's Identification Card

situated in Corona, New Mexico. Doty claimed to have seen the entire report detailing the incident, an assertion that carried weight due to his former position within the Air Force.

Dr. Steven Greer, The Disclosure Project

In stark contrast, Dr. Steven Greer entered the scene as a civilian outsider—a man who claimed to have been granted access to confidential information through his involvement with the Disclosure Project. Greer spoke of special access to unacknowledged programs that existed beyond the public's purview. He presented himself as an advocate for transparency, asserting that a higher level of knowledge regarding the crash was being withheld from the masses.

The narratives of Doty and Greer, while differing in substance, converged on one fundamental point: the veil of secrecy shrouding the Roswell incident. Doty's insider perspective hinted at the presence of classified information that he believes should now be presented for public scrutiny. Greer is one of the foremost authorities about UFOs, alien intelligence, and Unacknowledged Special Access Programs. To set the record straight from the cacophony of UFO "experts," he is also an advocate for the revelation of this hidden knowledge, asserting that humanity has the right to understand the full scope of what had transpired.

As we will see in chapter 10, their conflicting accounts cast a spotlight on the delicate balance between the need for national security and the desire for openness. As the years passed, the voices of Doty and Greer became intertwined with the wider narrative of Roswell, representing the tension between classified information and the quest for truth.

Right now I'm having amnesia and déjà vu at the same time. . .
I think I've forgotten this before.

—Steven Wright

Chapter 8

The Barney Barnett Revelation—The Unveiling of the San Agustin Plains

It was early July 1947. The San Agustin Plains stretched out like a forgotten canvas beneath the boundless New Mexico sky, each brushstroke of history waiting to be deciphered. Decades after the seismic events that reverberated from Roswell's epicenter, a new narrative thread emerged, weaving through time, eager to tug at the tapestry of secrets.

L. Grady "Barney" Barnett, an unassuming member of the Soil Conservation Department, became an unlikely purveyor of revelation. The air was charged with anticipation as Barette's truck traversed along the main highway, the horizon beckoning like a riddle waiting to be solved. And there it was—a shining metallic craft of unfamiliar design, lying just over a berm, an assemblage of materials beyond human understanding.

As Barney Barnett approached the mysterious craft and crash site, a scene reminiscent of an ancient ritual unfolded, as a congregation of professional archaeologists and impassioned enthusiasts descended upon the wreckage and Mr. Barnett within minutes. Their collective pulse quickened as they attempted to unearth the fragments of a cosmic puzzle, trying mentally to connect dots that transcended time and space. Metallic fragments scattered about, a spacecraft badly damaged, and bizarre humanoid occupants lay strewn around the crash site.

But as history has shown, curiosity often dances at the edge of power, and the line between disclosure and containment is a fine one. Government agents and military soldiers soon materialized, yelling to Barnette and the dig team to "move away, don't touch a thing." A veiled force from the unseen realms of authority cast a shroud of secrecy over the tableau. The enigma, it seemed, had guardians, and its secrets were meant to remain concealed.

The collision of inquiry and influence birthed a paradox—a mystery within a mystery. The very landscape that had witnessed the interplay of revelation and suppression seemed to hold its breath, as if aware of the hidden truths that lay within its grasp. Barnett's testimony lingered in the air, like a forgotten tune with the promise of forgotten chords.

As twilight painted the canvas of the plains, a profound convergence took place, an intersection of narratives where the sands of truth and deception intermingled, creating a mosaic that begged to be understood. Amidst the words spoken and unspoken, within the delicate dance of seekers and sentinels, the heart of the enigma pulsed, waiting for a dedicated soul to pull back the layers and expose the hidden mystery for the world to behold.

Although the above was a colorful interpretation of Mr. Barnett's story, we decided to add the intriguing account of Grady L. "Barney" Barnett's encounter with an otherworldly craft on the San Agustin Plains despite his story eventually being widely discredited by UFO researchers. Despite this contradiction, the decision to include this account in the narrative serves a larger purpose within the context of "Magdalena." It underscores the notion that even discredited or contested accounts can possess fragments of truth. While Barnett's story may not align entirely with the historical record, the fact that he and others like him have reported witnessing unusual phenomena should not be dismissed outright. Instead, these accounts can be viewed as pieces of a larger puzzle, contributing to the complexity and mystery of events like the Roswell incident.

Barnett's story was first introduced in 1980 in the publication *The Roswell Incident*. This account presented a narrative that aligned with the prevailing theories about extraterrestrial involvement in the famous Roswell incident. It was later discovered that Barney Barnett's wife had meticulously maintained a detailed diary chronicling the couple's activities during the pivotal year of 1947. Strikingly, this diary contained no mention of a crashed flying saucer on the San Agustin Plains.

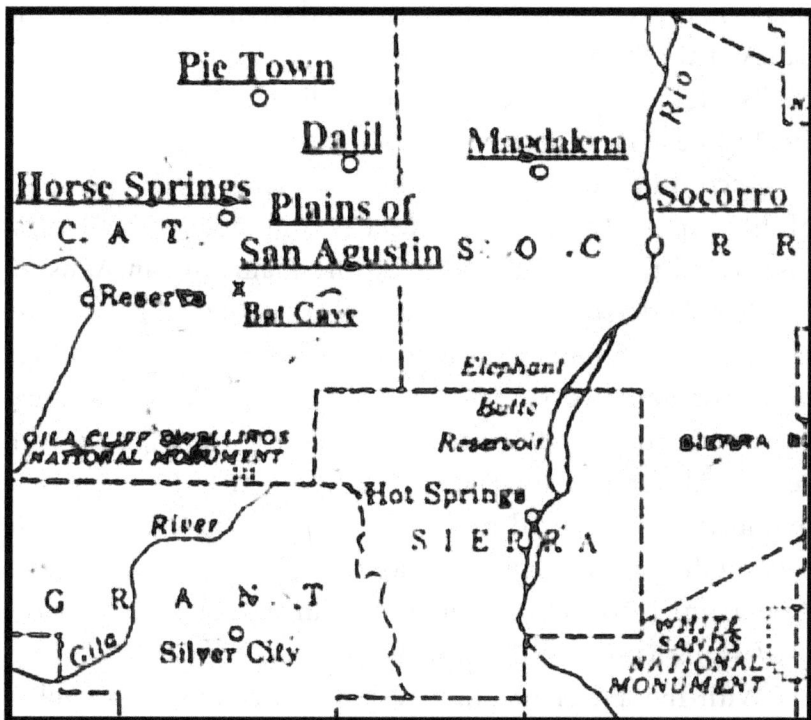

This glaring omission served as a challenge to the validity of Barnett's testimony, as it contradicted the very event he had described.

We thought it necessary to show the discrepancies between the testimonies and historical records; "Magdalena" encourages readers to critically evaluate the evidence, consider various perspectives, and draw their own conclusions about the events that transpired. The inclusion of Barney Barnett's account, despite the lack of corroboration in his wife's diary, serves as a reminder that uncovering the truth often requires sifting through a mix of credible and dubious information, all while remaining open to the possibility that hidden truths may exist beneath the surface.

Further complicating or corroborating the Barney Barnette story is the account from Gerald Anderson. Anderson was a small child, accompanying his father and family members on the San Agustin Plains in July of 1947.

The following transcript is taken directly from the March, 1992, issue of the *Skeptics UFO Newsletter*.

According to Anderson, he and four other members of his family (now all deceased)—and not Barnett—first discovered the crashed saucer on the Plains of San Agustin. Further, Anderson claimed that one of the four ETs was alive. Anderson said that a University of Pennsylvania archaeology professor and five students arrived and Anderson claimed the professor tried—unsuccessfully—to communicate in several different languages with the live ET. Regressive hypnosis administered by John S. Carpenter, MUFON state section director for southwest Missouri, was used to enhance Anderson's recollections, enabling him to remember that the professor's name was "Dr." Buskirk.

With the aid of Identikit techniques employed by police

to obtain a physical likeness of a criminal's face, Anderson was able to develop a sketch of Dr. Buskirk's appearance. Pro-UFOlogist Thomas J. Carey, who lives near the University of Philadelphia, volunteered to assist Friedman in trying to locate Dr. Buskirk, as he describes in a most interesting account published in the Nov./Dec. 1991 issue of *International UFO Reporter* (OUR). Thanks to a lot of hard work, and a book published by Dr. Winfred Buskirk, Carey managed to locate him in Albuquerque, New Mexico.

Exhibit 4. Gerald Anderson

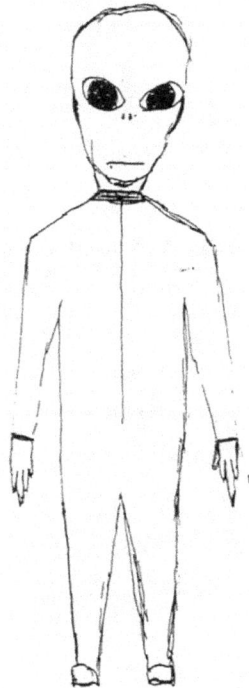

Exhibit 5. Gerald Anderson's sketch of the creature he saw on the Plains of San Agustin.

From Skeptics UFO Newsletter -- 1, a page showing Gerald Anderson and his drawing of the alien he claimed to see when taken to the purported crash site as a child.

In *Skeptics UFO Newsletter* -2- from March 1992, Buskirk flatly denied Anderson's tale. But he closely resembles the Identikit sketch that Anderson helped prepare, which might seem to confirm Anderson's story. Carey learned that Dr. Buskirk joined the faculty of the Albuquerque High School in 1950 and remained there until he retired in 1969. He taught American history and anthropology. By a curious coincidence, in the late 1960s, Gerald Anderson was a student at the same high school where Dr. Buskirk was teaching.

When Kevin Randle, who was suspicious of Anderson's tale, tried to obtain a transcript of Anderson's high school records to see if he had taken an anthropology course under Buskirk, Anderson cautioned school authorities not to release the information. However, Anderson himself obtained a transcript and provided what he purported to be a photocopy to John Carpenter—one of his staunchest supporters. In response to my query, Carpenter indicated that the photocopy he received from Anderson indicated that he had taken a course in sociology, not anthropology which Buskirk taught. But Anderson conceded that there was possible ambiguity in trying to read the photocopy made from microfilm.

On Oct. 7, I wrote Carpenter pointing out that "much hinges on the question of whether Gerald Anderson took a course in anthropology under Buskirk in 1957 or whether it was a course in sociology from another teacher." I then asked if Anderson would be willing "to authorize the current principal or the Albuquerque High School to carefully examine the original microfilm transcript and issue a public statement as to whether Anderson did, or did not, take a course in anthropology in 1957.

When Carpenter failed to respond, I wrote to him again on Nov. 27, but my second query also went unanswered.

On Jan. 5, 1992—nearly three months after I first wrote Carpenter—I wrote again to ask if he had passed along my Oct. 7 suggestion to Anderson and, if so, what was Anderson's response. Carpenter replied saying that my suggestion also had been made by Stan Friedman, Mark Rodeghier of the Hynek Center for UFO Studies, and Fred Whiting of the Fund for UFO Research "even before you suggested this." (Great minds run in similar channels.)

What was Anderson's reaction to this suggestion? He would think it over before deciding. Carpenter explained: "Gerald doesn't care what anybody thinks at the present time." I responded on Jan. 13, and asked Carpenter: "If Anderson sought your advice, would you suggest that he ought to agree to the proposal to prove his veracity?" Carpenter replied: "He did, and I did."

Question: Why is Anderson so reluctant to let an independent authority examine his high school transcript to determine whether or not he took a course under Dr. Buskirk? And why did Friedman continue to endorse the veracity of Anderson's crashed saucer tale?

Nothing good ever happens after midnight.

Chapter 9

A Salacious Night and a Glowing Object— The Jim Ragsdale Saga

Roswell authors Kevin Randle of Iowa and Donald Schmitt of Wisconsin plunged into their Roswell Crash Event research, driven by an insatiable curiosity to uncover the truth hidden beneath the layers of secrecy. The more they dug, the more they discovered what we hope to convey in this book—that the Roswell incident was not a singular event, but part of a wider tapestry woven with tales of other potential UFO recoveries.

Their pursuit led them to a source who hinted at another location, one situated much closer to Roswell than previously acknowledged. The coordinates pointed to a spot just 30 miles north by northwest of town, a discreet marker off U.S. Highway 285.

That source was a former oil field worker named Jim Ragsdale. Ragsdale had toiled in the depths of the earth, where darkness and grit were constants. At 66 years old, he was nearing the end of his journey, battling lung cancer, and tethered to a respirator, an unexpected consequence of an industrial accident. Time was slipping through his grasp like sand, and he seemed compelled to share a truth that had haunted him for decades.

It was in the crisp air of January 1993 that Schmitt knocked on

Ragsdale's door. With each labored breath, Ragsdale recounted a story that bordered on the unbelievable, transcending the wildest imaginings of his interviewer. His words echoed through the air, filling the room with a mixture of awe and uncertainty. An affidavit, a piece of paper that would etch his words into permanence, lay before him, awaiting his signature. With resolute determination, Ragsdale signed his name, as if sealing a pact with history.

This is the story he affirmed:

In the depths of a sultry July night in 1947, Ragsdale and a woman found themselves in the back of his pick-up truck, free-spirited and unburdened. The world around them was vast, and the night held the promise of secrets yet unveiled. Then, a flash, bright and searing, pierced the darkness, followed by an otherworldly light that cast an ethereal glow upon the landscape. It was an encounter that defied logic, an event that would forever define Ragsdale's existence.

As dawn painted the sky with hues of gold and amber, Ragsdale and his companion followed a trail that led them to a site that would forever be etched in their memories. Debris, unlike anything terrestrial, lay scattered like fragments of a shattered reality. And there, amidst the wreckage, were beings unlike any Ragsdale had ever seen—smaller in stature, enigmatic in form.

Ragsdale's two-page affidavit, succinct yet laden with the weight of history, recounted the location: "approximately 40 miles northwest of Roswell." The coordinates themselves were cryptic, leaving room for ambiguity. Yet, Randle and Schmitt were not content to rely solely on words; they had meticulously documented the new site with photographs, capturing a glimpse of a place that held secrets beyond imagination.

During an interview preserved on tape, Ragsdale identified the location with certainty, tracing lines on photographs that bridged the gap between his words and the reality he had experienced. His trembling hand, a testament to the frailty of human existence, pointed to a truth that had eluded the world for decades.

Randle and Schmitt understood the gravity of what they had uncovered. Jim Ragsdale's account was a testament to the enduring power of testimony, a thread that wove through time to reveal a mosaic of events shrouded in secrecy. With unwavering dedication, they pressed on, driven by a desire to peel back the layers of history, to uncover what lay beneath the surface, and to bring to light the fragments of truth scattered within the enigma of the unknown.

Let us take a better look at the Ragsdale case. The following transcript was taken from the RoswellFiles.com website, which has respectability amongst UFO researchers, including myself.

(Note: We have edited some parts for brevity.)

Jim Ragsdale's first Crash Site: (This is the site, now owned by Miller "Hub" Corn, which was originally owned by the McKnight family. It is about 35 miles north-by-northwest of Roswell.)

Jim Ragsdale was a truck driver living in Carlsbad at the time of the Roswell incident. His story begins:

"We (Jim and his girlfriend, the aptly named Trudy Truelove) were lying in the back of my pickup truck, buck naked, drinking beer and having a good ol' time when all hell broke loose."

About 11:30 p.m., Ragsdale said he saw an object roar overhead and slam into the ground a mile or so from where Ragsdale was entertaining his young companion.

After the rain ended Ragsdale and his girlfriend got and drove across the rocky terrain to the edge of a short cliff. Using a flashlight in which the batteries were failing, they saw a ship stuck in the side of the cliff. As the flashlight was failing, they decided to go back to where they had been and to return in the morning.

Why they never decided to drive the relatively short distance to town to report the crash and to try to get aid for any possible survivors has never really been answered.

When the sun came up, Ragsdale and Trudy Truelove left where they had been parking and returned to the cliff to examine the crash site. Ragsdale and Truelove then got their first good look at the scene and, according to Ragsdale, Truelove wanted to "get the hell out of there." They went down and examined some of the debris that was lying all over the ground and marveled at the characteristics. "You could take that stuff and wad it up and it would straighten itself out." Near the craft, Ragsdale saw "bodies or something laying there. They looked like bodies. They weren't very long . . . four or five feet long at most."

Ragsdale and Truelove didn't check to see if any of them were alive or in need of help. They decided instead to gather up some of the wreckage and were throwing it into their truck when they "heard all of them coming. . . It was two or three six-by-six Army trucks, a wrecker and everything. Leading the pack was a '47 Ford car with guys in it. MPs in it."

While they watched, the trucks fanned out and parked. Now Ragsdale said he got worried along with Truelove. He pulled his truck (or was it a Jeep?) into a gathering of trees and watched as the MPs began to cordon off the area. They watched long enough to know that "they cleaned everything all up. I mean they cleaned it. They raked the ground and everything."

Ragsdale and Truelove decided to get out before the MPs searched the area and returned to the site of their amorous adventures of the night before.

So, according to Ragsdale's story, the MPs and the other soldiers cleaned up everything, including, apparently, the bodies, and raked the ground prior to searching the area.

Although Ragsdale is one of Randle's and Schmitt's star witnesses, and said he was at or near the crash site until the Army cleaned it up, he never mentioned seeing any archaeologists prior to the Army's arrival. Yet, Randle and Schmitt insist that the archaeologists arrived prior to the Army.

Researcher & writer
Donald R. Schmitt

What About the Debris?

Since Ragsdale took some of the debris, why can't it be tested? In his most recent sworn statement, Ragsdale claims:

"Unexplained to this day is the disappearance of the material. My friend (Trudy Truelove) had some in her vehicle when (many months later) she was killed hitting a bridge and it was gone when the wreckage was brought into town. My truck and trailer was (sic) stolen from my home, again with material in the truck, never to be heard from anywhere. My home was broken into, completely ransacked, and what was taken was material, a gun and very little else of value."

As time went on, Ragsdale's story altered some. In his early tale, he hadn't looked inside the craft or known how many bodies were there. But now, he claims he looked inside and tried to remove their helmets. In other versions of his tale, he took a whole load of "golden helmets" from the scene and buried them. The number of these "golden helmets" varied somewhat. Jim cannot remember where he buried these helmets, however— another "mystery" that lingers on.

Jim Finds a New Crash Site

On April 15, 1995, Ragsdale signed another affidavit in which he totally changed where the alien spaceship was supposed to have crashed. He moved the crash site from 35 miles north of Roswell to another location roughly 55 miles west of Roswell.

He also made significant changes from his first affidavit, beyond merely changing the location of the impact site.

So what do the neighbors say?

The family of the people who owned the ranch during the period when the crash supposedly happened disputes Jim Ragsdale's first crash site (the "Hub" Corn site).

In a sworn statement made on Feb. 3, 1997, Jim McKnight notes that the "alleged impact site is located on a part of the ranch that belonged to my aunt and is a little over a mile west of my grandfather's original ranch house. . . . I do not believe that a UFO or anything else crashed at the alleged crash site in 1947 for several reasons. No one in my family had any knowledge of such a crash or military retrieval. If a coyote crossed that ranch, my dad or uncle would likely see his tracks. . . I cannot believe that a convoy of Army trucks and cars could have come and gone without them noticing. If they had seen it, they would have told us about it."

To reach the supposed crash site, the Army would have had

to pass within 200 yards of the ranch house on land owned by McKnight's family.

McKnight continued, "During the 1950s I rode horseback all over both pastures around the alleged crash site on a number of different occasions."

Why did he ride horseback? ". . . [B]ecause there were not any roads west from the ranch house [to the alleged impact site]. It was not until the early 1960s that my aunt hired a bulldozer to build a crossing on the Macho (an arroyo)."

In a later interview, when asked if an Army convoy could have made it, McKnight replied "to get to the alleged impact site a convoy would have to get across the Macho which was all but impossible in 1947."

His affidavit concludes "the entire Roswell Incident has been of great interest to me and I hope to find the truth some day, I do not have an ax to grind nor a profit to be made from this incident."

(Affidavit available from the Roswell International UFO Museum which obtained it initially)

What about the second Roswell Crash Site of Jim Ragsdale?

Albuquerque journalist William P. Barrett researched the Roswell Incident for an article for the July 15, 1996, issue of *Forbes* magazine (which was headlined: "Unidentified Flying Dollars") and an article for the Albuquerque newspaper *Crosswinds*. Barrett interviewed people who had lived near the Ragsdale impact site. From the *Crosswinds* article:

- Dorothy Epps, whose family-owned land is only one half mile from the Ragsdale site: "I'm quite sure we would have heard about it if it were true. It's all a hoax."

- Bill Edgar, who worked as a farm hand near the Ragsdale site

41

in 1947: "It never happened. I never heard about saucers or soldiers moving around."

- Kenny Schear, manager of the nearby Armstrong ranch who arrived in 1955: I've talked to all the old-timers over the years. I think it's the biggest damned joke I've ever heard."

Barrett also interviewed Ragsdale's former wife. Vennie Scott, who divorced him after 40 years of marriage, said that he had never told her about a crashed saucer, but she said she once heard her husband, while drunk, tell the tale to a friend. Yet, Randle and Schmitt, in their second book on Roswell, reported that one of the reasons for believing Ragsdale was that his wife Mary corroborated his story.

Some more doubts creep in

It seems that Randle has since decided that Ragsdale isn't as credible as he once thought. From the United Kingdom UFO Network, April 11, 1998, IRC meeting on #UFO, in response to the question: "Who do you think is the least credible of the Roswell witnesses and why?" Kevin Randle replied: "Jim Ragsdale changed his story. . ."

In a time of universal deceit—telling the truth is a revolutionary
act.

—Origin uncertain (attributed to Antonio Gramsci)

Chapter 10

Unveiling the Testimonies

Let us now move forward to the present day to expand the
narrative to encompass the voices of individuals who had
encountered the enigma of Roswell from different vantage
points. Richard M. Doty, with his assertion of insider knowledge,
and Dr. Steven Greer, with his advocacy for disclosure, highlighted
the ongoing struggle to decipher the truth beneath layers of
secrecy. As their accounts mingled with the broader discourse,
the question of what lay beyond the official narrative deepened,
casting a shadow of intrigue over an already enigmatic tale.

As the Roswell narrative continued to unfold, new voices
emerged to add depth and complexity to the tapestry of mystery.
As noted in chapter 7, Richard M. Doty, a former special agent
with the Air Force Office of Special Investigations, and Dr. Steven
Greer of the Disclosure Project stepped into the spotlight, each
offering their unique perspectives on the events surrounding the
enigmatic incident.

Their testimonies presented contrasting viewpoints,
reflecting the broader dichotomy between classified information
and the pursuit of transparency. Doty's insider insights and
Greer's claims of special access to unacknowledged programs
cast a shadow of intrigue over the ongoing quest to uncover the
truth behind the Roswell crash.

Their accounts intersect with the narrative, inviting a deeper exploration of the enigma through their respective lenses. The following pages hold their words, their perspectives, and their convictions, weaving an intricate web of testimony that beckons us to probe further into the heart of the Roswell mystery.

The following testimony is taken directly from Dr. Steven Greer's appearance on Vlad TV:

The Roswell crash absolutely happened; before they passed away, I had known some of the men who were there at the Roswell Base. But Roswell was not the first crash; there actually was (sic) a few crash retrieval events in the late '30s. We know at the Trinity site in 1945 shortly after we detonated the bomb, a craft came down in that area that we retrieved. But the Roswell event is the most celebrated. There were actually three extra-terrestrial crafts involved. We have a document shown in my book *Unacknowledged* that describes a radar system that the government had put in at Roswell.

Let me tell you about the military speak [sic]. A radar system we think about is one that bounces radar off the skin of an aircraft or object. Those systems can also have a directed energy warfare system attached to it or associated with it, either within the system or very nearby. So that when something is "painted" or tracked by radar it can also be hit by an electromagnetic weapon. Those systems were being experimented with in the '30s and '40s, and by 1947, this FBI document from a field agent to J. Edgar Hoover, which we have published, states that the electromagnetic weapon was "switched on" so the Roswell radar had to have more than a radar component—it had to have an electromagnetic component to it. And there were three of these E.T. craft over that area, two of them collided and one was in a zillion pieces not far from Roswell Army Air base, the other continued Westward towards Socorro, NM, impacted and broke and there were extra-terrestrial bodies and one living E.T. was taken from that crash site.

The third craft wasn't found until I believe in 1951 up in mountains going way northwest from Roswell. The one E.T. survivor was last seen by an Army Intelligence guy I known (sic) to see the being in 1951 at Camp Perry in Virginia. It was in a crate wearing boxer shorts. It didn't live much longer, about four years in captivity.

The following transcript is from Richard Doty on the Sirius Disclosure Project, ironically, being interviewed by Dr. Greer.

Author's Note: Since the foremost authority, with military credentials, willing to discuss the two Roswell crashes is Richard Doty, and that he specifically mentions the two craft being identical, we have chosen, for brevity's sake, to use the detailed description of the Corona crash in reference also to the Magdalena/

Richard M. Doty, former investigatory officer with the U.S. Air Force Office of Special Investigations

Horse Peak craft. Because of Richard Doty's military journey, he was specifically asked to be the technical expert on the second crash site, which in Mr. Doty's opinion, has been misrepresented and mistranslated for over seventy years.

My name is Richard Doty and I was assigned as a Special Agent with the Air Force Office of Special Investigations at Kirkland AFB, while I was a Counterintelligence Officer assigned to the base, and during my time there, the first few months, I was briefed into a Special Access Program involving the United States government's investigation and contact with extra-terrestrials and the visitation of these extra-terrestrials to earth. And the Air Force's involvement with these extra-terrestrials. And during this time I conducted investigations not just involving the UFO phenomenon, but my primary mission, probably sixty percent of my time, dealt with that; investigating any UFO sightings and any threat or threats imposed by these extra-terrestrials on the Air Force or Air Force property.

I was read into this project in the summer of 1979. The briefing was, it was a Special Access Program that had special security clearance to have access to it and I was briefed into it by an Air Force Colonel from Washington, D.C., who came down and briefed myself and a couple of other people into this program. I'll leave the Coronel's name out of it.

There are still some classifications involved in this, but the code name I was briefed into was called Yankee Black. That was the program's briefing, not necessarily the UFO program's name; it was actually a security code for an access program. Yankee White was [sic] access to the President of the United States, the White House. And Yankee Black was the access you would have to have to get into this program or read into the program.

The briefing started out with the government's

involvement with these beings, and it started out with the crash at Roswell. But actually, the crash didn't happen at Roswell, it happened closer to Corona, New Mexico. Southwest of Corona, New Mexico. And a second crash site that occurred in Magdalena or Horse Mesa, west of Magdalena in New Mexico. Which wasn't located like the Roswell crash in '47, the crash in Magdalena wasn't located until about '49. They showed us a movie, I believe a 16mm movie, on the recovery. The narrator of the movie, obviously the movie was classified, the narrator of the movie detailed when the crashed occurred, approximately when the crash (Corona) occurred in the later part of June, in 1947, and the recovery showing military personnel at the recovery site, recovering the bodies at the site and the craft that was at that site, and one live extra-terrestrial was found live at that site.

And we were told that the extra-terrestrial was taken to Kirkland Field Air Force Base at that time and then on to Los Alamos for some time. It didn't explain fully in the move what happened to that extra-terrestrial, but it did explain that it died, I believe it was 1952. But the bodies (deceased) found at the site were placed in a deep freeze and sent to Wright-Pat[terson] Airfield in Dayton, Ohio.

The craft was more or less an oval or egg-shaped craft, it wasn't saucer shape. The creatures were about four foot and some of the creatures were mangled or heavily injured and their bodies were torn apart but two of the bodies were pretty much intact. I am not sure of an autopsy, but they (the narrator) didn't discuss that. But the creatures were approximately four foot, they didn't appear to have any ears, had a detention for a nose, really big eyes and a tight-fitting suit, almost looked like they were nude but did have a suit on. Four fingers, suction devices on the tips of their four fingers and um one of them had a head apparatus device on it maybe a helmet, earphone or some type of device that could communicate with the craft or something else.

They found a number of different objects in the craft that they used and experimented with. They found a piece of plexiglass or that they thought was Plexi-glass, a rectangle piece of Plexi-glass that they experimented with for years until they found out that it was an energy device for the craft.

Then they showed us the craft recovery in 1949 in Horse Mesa (Magdalena/Horse Peak/Luera Mountain Base) THAT craft crashed at the same time as the '47 crash but because of the remoteness of the location it wasn't detected until a rancher found it on his property in '49. And they did a recovery op, project on that craft but the bodies were decayed and there wasn't much left of them (ET bodies) but THAT craft was the same type of craft found in Corona, an oval shaped craft, but had damage to it much like the one at Corona did. And I think the opinion of the scientists was that the two craft had crashed. And I think nobody has it right. One of things, one of things that is quite disgusting for the people who have ever been briefed into these programs is that there is not much out there that's actual factual. The UFO community disinforms itself; people go out there and write books, without any facts, ninety percent of the people who go out and write these books, these authors have never been in the military or worked in the intelligence community, never had a security clearance and there are just relying on second, third, fourth hand information to write a book. And poison the readers and the rest of the UFOP community.

So, the July crash actually crashed [sic] in the end of June, the recovery project was into July because it was at the end of June, and people just didn't get it right. And the UFO community didn't get it right. Now there are some people out there that have tried to present the facts, but they have been ridiculed and so their information is not being believed. Just like the Horse Mesa (Horse Peak) crash (recovery) in '49, very few people have that factual, they think it was an entirely different craft. They think it was a different craft than Corona craft, but it was the exactly (sic) same (type) of vehicle . . . exactly the same.

And the damages, they showed in this movie they showed sketches of the crafts together at some location, and it appeared to anybody with a logical mind could see that these crafts crashed together; why they crashed I was never told, I believe the EBEN they called this particular entity that lived, the EBEN he probably explained but I was never briefed into exactly what happened what he or how he explained that the two craft crashed. I know it was a lightning storm, it was a storm in that time period that it crashed. But the two crashes have been separated by some people and discounted by others within the UFO community. And that's what is so disgusting and troubling in the UFO community, that's why I have nothing to do with them anymore. I've tried, I went to UFO conventions and tried to explain what the truth is because nobody wants to hear you because they've written a book that says it happened this way and they aren't gonna listen to you even though they really do know the truth.

Dr. Greer responds, "Right, don't bother me with the facts, my mind is made up."

Remember that Doty continues that the crafts of both crashes were (according to Doty's briefing of the government film) identical:

It was about 35 foot in diameter across 35 by 40 something life that, it didn't have any actual levers or flight control systems that we identify as flight control systems or any avionics that we would identify as avionics. Totally unknown devices in the craft the steering mechanisms, but they eventually over time figured it out. And it was done all by hand, the creatures would put their hands on controls, and they would have these headsets on, and this headset would somehow help them control the craft. And the avionics, the very very sophisticated avionics took us years I think to figure out. And I was never briefed into that so I can't talk, I don't know about any of that or what they figured out. They took the crafts to Wright-Patterson, at the time, in the late '40s was probably the best place to understand or to try and figure out the had the best scientists there to figure out that these crafts flew."

There was much more to this interview between Richard Doty and Dr. Steven Greer, but here we are only focusing on Doty's testimony of the Roswell Crash Event.

In the next chapters, let us return to Roswell and read the accounts of other witnesses who claim to have found additional crashes that unfolded in July of '47.

Centerfold

Maps & Images

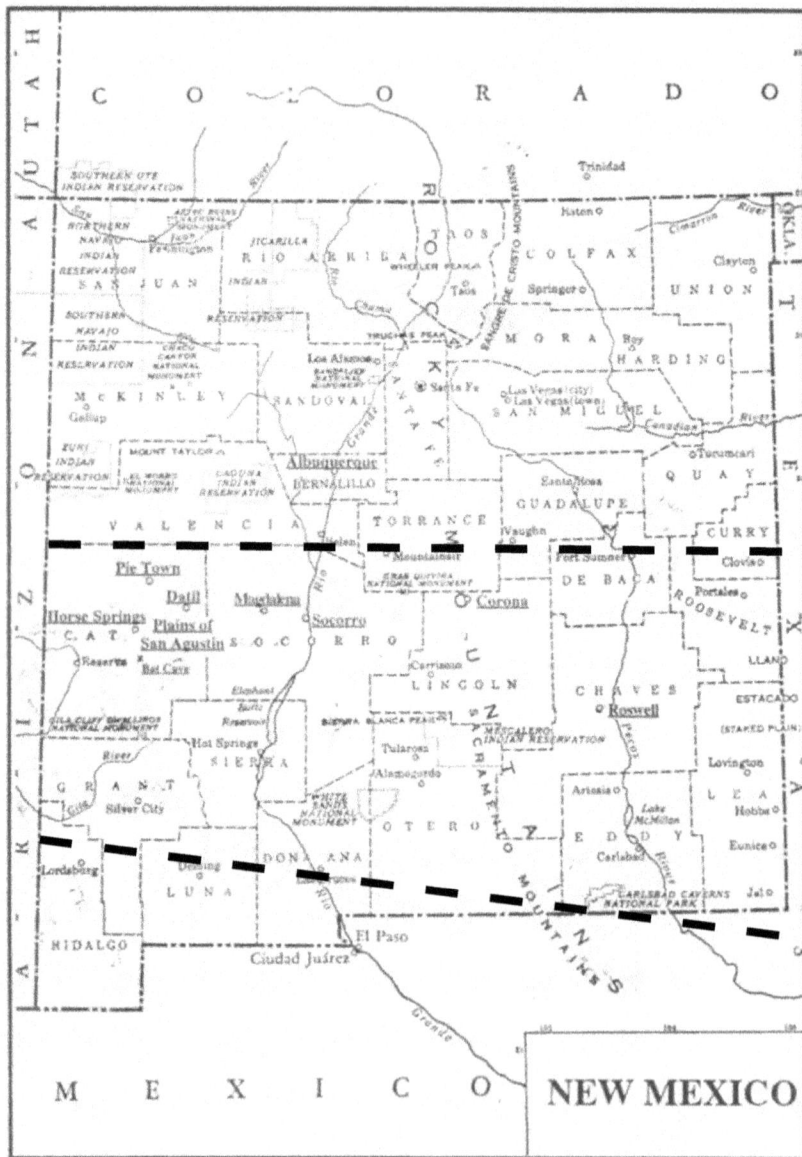

Exhibit 1. New Mexico.

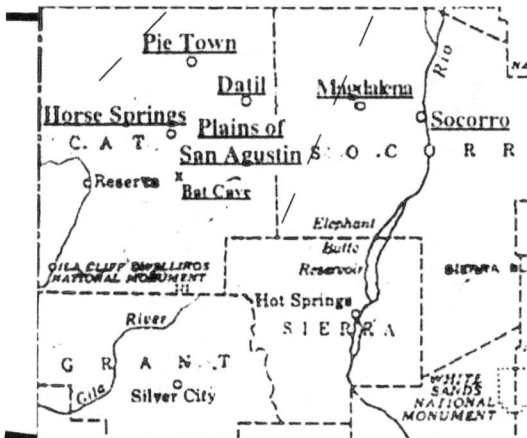

Approximate location of Magdalena crash
site in southwestern New Mexico

The town of Magdalena, New Mexico, in the 1920s, approximately two decades before the reported crash of a pair of alien ships nearby.

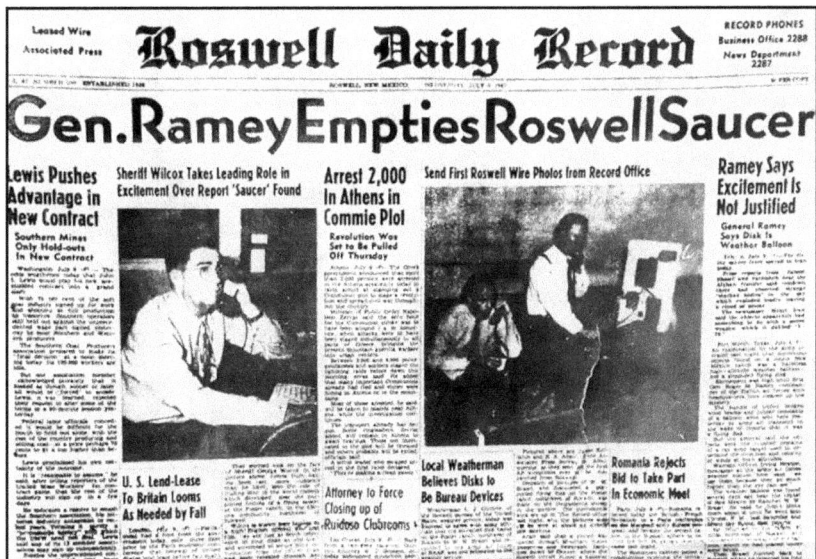

This image shows the front page of the *Roswell* (NM) *Daily Record*, July 5, 1947, that headlined the crash of suspected UFOs in the desert nearby. While reporting the fact of the crash, the newsppaer also published the "official line" about what exactly had crashlanded. Note three headline columns: "**Sheriff Wilcox Takes Leading Role in Excitement over Report 'Saucer' Found**," just above the photograph on the left; below the second photo, "**Local Weatherman Believes Disk to Be Bureau Devices**"; and on the top-right-hand column, the official story that "**Ramey Says Excitement is Not Justified: General Ramey Says Disk Is Weather Balloon**."

Roswell
(1 page)

TELETYPE

FBI DALLAS   7-8-47   6-17 PM

DIRECTOR AND SAC, CINCINNATI   URGENT

FLYING DISC, INFORMATION CONCERNING.   HEADQUARTERS

EIGHTH AIR FORCE, TELEPHONICALLY ADVISED THIS OFFICE THAT AN OBJECT
PURPORTING TO BE A FLYING DISC WAS RE COVERED NEAR ROSWELL, NEW
MEXICO, THIS DATE. THE DISC IS HEXAGONAL IN SHAPE AND WAS SUSPENDED
FROM A BALLON BY CABLE, WHICH BALLON WAS APPROXIMATELY TWENTY
FEET IN DIAMETER.   FURTHER ADVISED THAT THE OBJECT
FOUND RESEMBLES A HIGH ALTITUDE WEATHER BALLOON WITH A RADAR
REFLECTOR, BUT THAT TELEPHONIC CONVERSATION BETWEEN THEIR OFFICE
AND WRIGHT FIELD HAD NOT BORNE OUT THIS BELIEF. DISC AND
BALLOON BEING TRANSPORTED TO WRIGHT FIELD BY SPECIAL PLANE FOR EXAMINATI
INFORMATION PROVIDED THIS OFFICE BECAUSE OF NATIONAL INTEREST IN CASE .
AND FACT THAT NATIONAL BROADCASTING COMPANY, ASSOCIATED PRESS, AND
OTHERS ATTEMPTING TO BREAK STORY OF LOCATION OF DISC TODAY.
ADVISED WOULD REQUEST WRIGHT FIELD TO ADVISE CINCINNATI
OFFICE RESULTS OF EXAMINATION. NO FURTHER INVESTIGATION BEING
CONDUCTED.

WYLY
RECORDED
END
C:XXX ACK IN ORDER
UA 92 FBI C1 MJW
DPI NS
8-38 PM O
6-22 PM OK FBI WASH DC
OK FBI OR

The teletyped cable from the FBI Dallas office to the Director of
the Strategic Air Command in Cincinnati, Ohio, concerning the
crashed "flying disc" being sent to Wright Field (now Wright-
Patterson Air Force Base) in Dayton, Ohio, for investigation. Note
the assertion, already official, that what had crashed was a "high
altitude weather balloon with a radar reflector."

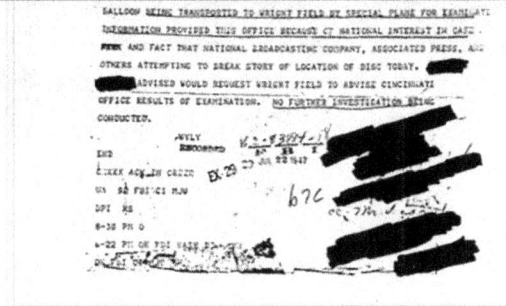

This document is available on the FBI website in their FOIA library known as The Vault. Several more FBI investigations of UFOs conducted from 1947 to 1954 are also included in The Vault.

PROJECT BLUE BOOK

From 1947 to 1969, a total of 12,618 sightings of UFOs were collected and investigated by the U.S. Air Force. The project, known as Project BLUE BOOK, was headquartered at Wright-Patterson Air Force Base in Dayton, Ohio.

As a result of several private and governmental investigations and studies conducted during this time period, the members of the Air Force running Project BLUE BOOK reached the following conclusions:

- No UFO reported, investigated, and evaluated by the Air Force had ever given any indication of threat to our national security.

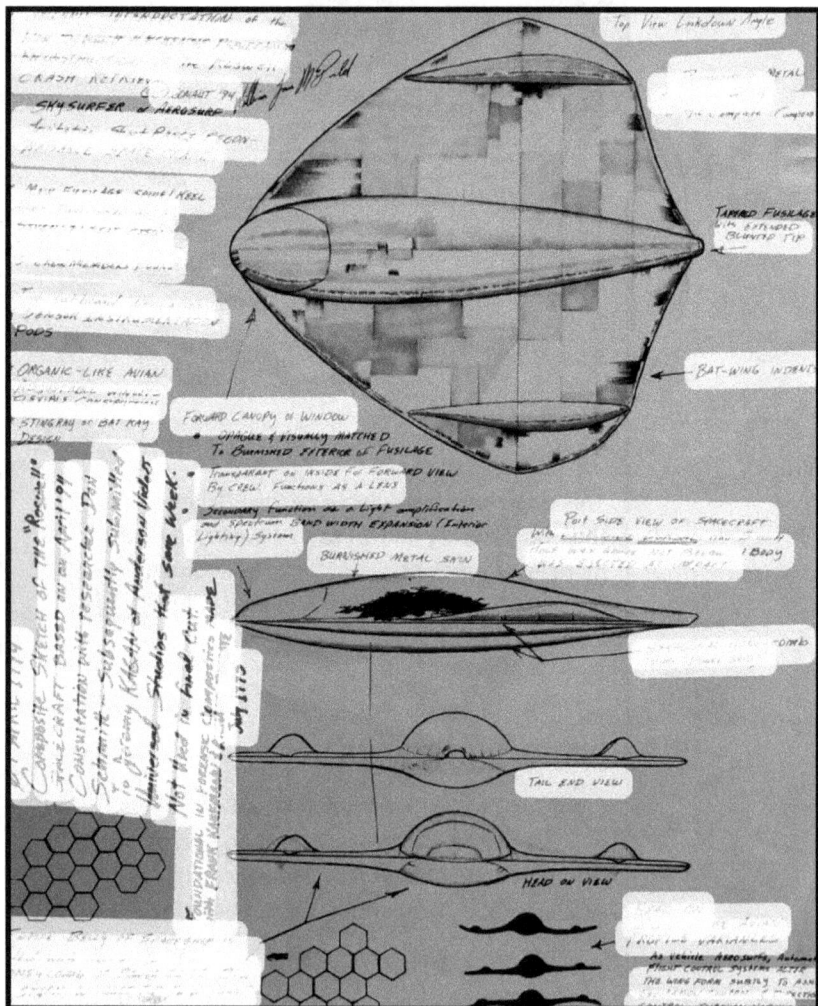

Drawing and schematic by Kevin D. Randle, Donald R. Schmitt, and William Louis McDonald, ©1995

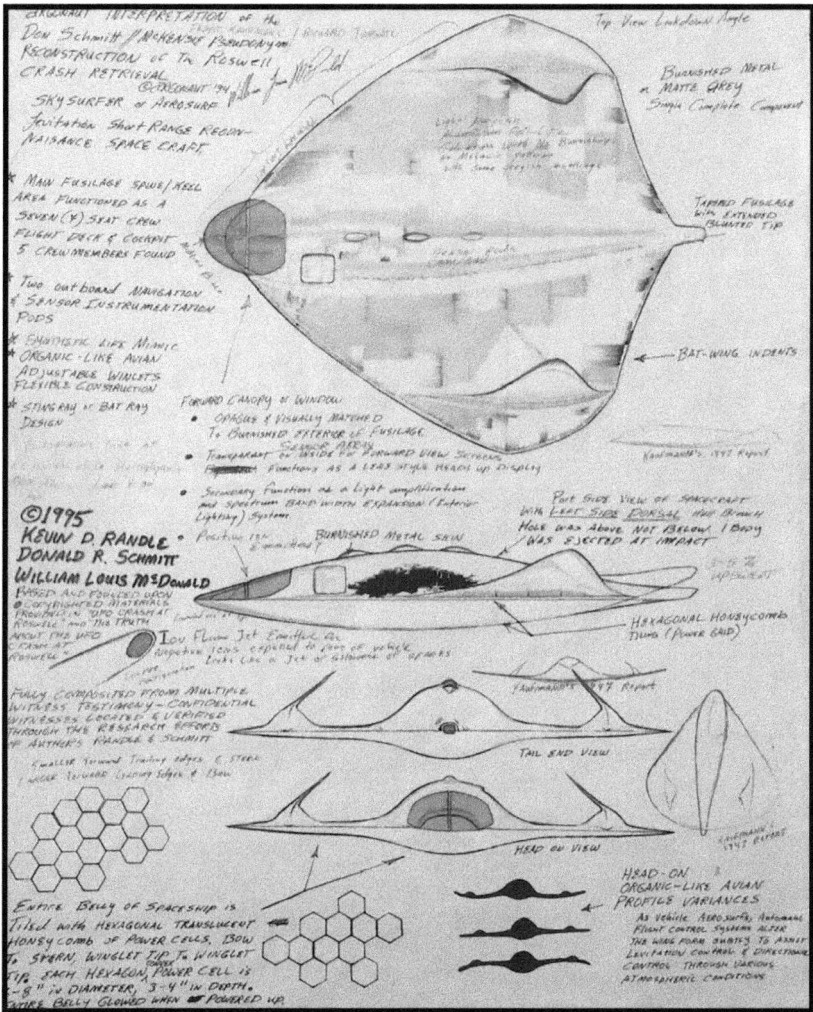

Chapter 11

Wendelle C. Stevens: What or Who Are the Grey Beings?

Wendelle Stevens is a name relatively unknown to the general public, but within the world of UFO enthusiasts and researchers, he was a prominent figure. Born in 1923, Stevens had an unconventional journey that led him into the realms of UFOlogy and the quest for answers regarding extraterrestrial life. His contributions to the field would forever change the way we perceive the phenomenon of alleged alien visitations.

In the early 1960s, Wendelle Stevens found himself drawn to the mysteries of unidentified flying objects. His military background as a lieutenant colonel in the United States Air Force served as a catalyst for his interest in UFOs. As he delved deeper into the subject, Stevens became a prolific author, documenting cases and encounters that defied conventional explanations. His work would eventually lead him to a groundbreaking revelation, one that linked the Roswell incident to a broader narrative involving a species known as the Greys.

Stevens's claims, as featured in the documentary UFO Chronicles: Aliens on Earth, produced by Gravitas Ventures, presented a unique perspective on the Roswell incident and the beings associated with it. According to Stevens, the Greys were not only involved in the Roswell event but had been visiting Earth since the 1960s. These visitors, hailing from a distant planet orbiting two parallel suns known as Reticulum, challenged the very definition of life as we know it.

One of the most striking aspects of Stevens's claims was his assertion that the Greys were non-placental creatures. Unlike mammals, they lacked gastrointestinal organs and distinguishable sexual organs, leading to a profound mystery regarding their reproductive processes. This enigma extended to their very nature—were they animals, a separate species altogether, or something entirely beyond our comprehension?

The implications of these claims were profound. If true, they indicated that the Greys were not just visitors from another world but a different order of life, possessing a morphology and biology that defied earthly norms. The notion of a hybrid being, born from a planet bathed in the light of twin suns, challenged the boundaries of what we considered possible.

While skepticism surrounded Stevens's assertions, his dedication to unraveling the mysteries of extraterrestrial life was

Lieutenant Colonel Wendelle C. Stevens in his U.S. Air Force officer's uniform.

undeniable. He became a trailblazer in the world of UFOlogy, sparking discussions and debates that continue to this day. Wendelle Stevens, a man who had once been a military officer, was now a respected voice in the pursuit of understanding what lies beyond our planet.

As the years passed, the legacy of Wendelle Stevens and his claims lived on, etching their place in the annals of UFO research. His unyielding curiosity and willingness to challenge conventional thinking remind us that, in the vast universe, the answers to our most profound questions may be stranger and more incredible than we ever imagined.

In all chaos there is a cosmos, in all disorder a secret order.

—Carl Jung

Chapter 12

Secret Weapon—A Colonel's Tale of Military Intelligence and Weaponry

I n the twilight of secrecy, a new figure steps forward, Colonel Richard French, a man bound by his allegiance to intelligence and compelled by the weight of truth. As his time on this earthly stage draws to a close, Colonel French takes pen to paper, chronicling a narrative that transcends the boundaries of official accounts. In his book, revelations cascade like ripples through the annals of history, painting a narrative that adds layers to the Roswell enigma, while shedding light on the depths of human ingenuity.

A verified pilot with the USAF, Colonel French's voice is both a whisper and a thunderclap, resonating with the gravity of a lifetime of service. In his accounts, a new dimension emerges— one of not one, but two crashes in the New Mexico landscape. The revelation resonates with an eerie resonance, echoing the whispers of witness accounts that have traversed decades. His words beckon us to confront the complexity of these events, challenging the notion of singularity.

Within the pages of his narrative, a plot unfolds that transcends the bounds of imagination—an experimental aircraft from White Sands emerges as a protagonist, wielding the power of the electronic pulse weapon to engage, disable and bring down an unidentified flying craft. Did the skies above New Mexico bear witness to a clash between innovation and the unknown—a battle of technology and cosmic forces? The narrative, in its audacity, paints a portrait of a dual encounter, one shaped by human determination and the other by cosmic happenstance.

Col. Richard French, USAF (ret.)

As Colonel French's story unfurls, it unveils a complex web of intrigue. The electronic pulse weapon, a creation of human hands, serves as a harbinger of a new era—a realm where technology wields the power to engage with the enigmatic realms beyond our world. The narrative underscores humanity's audacious reach, bridging the gap between the ordinary and the extraordinary, while hinting at the intricate dance between our species and the cosmic mysteries that surround us.

In the closing chapters of his life, Colonel French, who has stirred the UFO pot before with tales of an underwater UFO, beckons us to revisit our understanding of the Roswell events. His narrative casts a dual light on the landscape, where the skies bore witness to more than one enigmatic encounter. As we navigate the pages of his revelations, we find ourselves in a realm where human ambition and cosmic forces intersect, leaving us to ponder the depths of truth that have remained shrouded for generations. The echoes of Colonel French's words remind us that the universe, like the enigma of Roswell, is a tapestry woven with threads of complexity, waiting for those willing to unravel its mysteries.

In developing this book, I had a phone call with Army Colonel John Alexander—a phone call that went "sideways" rather quickly. John is a retired colonel in the United States Army, where he worked with Army Intelligence, as an Inspector General and as the Director of the US Army Advanced Concepts Lab. After leaving the army, John worked as the Program Manager for Non-Lethal Defense at Los Alamos National Laboratory. He is now a prominent non-lethal weapons expert and consultant.

Col. Alexander has expressed skepticism about French's assertions. In fact, he has emphatically dismissed them, stating to numerous media outlets, saying "There is absolutely no possibility. None whatsoever."

He continued, "During the 1980s, I spearheaded the development of cutting-edge pulse-power weaponry. Even at that point, such technology was beyond our reach. In the 1960s, we experimented with laser systems, but their operational scope was severely restricted, and operational laser weaponry was far from being a reality at that time."

The question remains, like Doty, why would a USAF pilot and counterintelligence agent back up accounts that UFOs are off-planet craft? One has to ask oneself, what is the reason other than an end-of-life catharsis, which is a real psychological effect on some people who hold life-long secrets.

No legacy is so rich as honesty.

—William Shakespeare

Chapter 13

Bridging the Years—A 2023 Reaffirmation of Roswell from Richard Doty

This is a reaffirmation of the basic account of the entire Roswell Crash Event, as told in August of 2023 by Richard Doty to this author.

An archeologist team from the University of New Mexico was near Corona and located a crashed aircraft in early July 1947, which contained four dead alien bodies and one live alien. The archeologist notified the local sheriff and the New Mexico State Police, who eventually notified the U.S. Military. The live alien was transported to Kirkland Field and eventually taken to Los Alamos, which had a facility to retain it. This alien was named EBEN #1. It was around 1952. It communicated first with hand signals and then scientists were able to attach a device to its vocal cords which gave the being the ability to talk.

In 1949, a rancher in Catron County, 10 miles from Magdalena, near the western base of the Luera Mountains was moving his cattle to a higher grazing area when he came upon a crash site on top of the Luera Mountain. The rancher eventually contacted the Catron County Sheriff eleven days later. It took the sheriff another six days to travel to the crash site. The sheriff took some photographs and contacted the US Air Force at Kirkland Field. It took another 21 days for the Air Force to respond and recover the crash site and the five bodies.

After scientists analyzed the incident, it was revealed that the two crafts were identical. The bodies were identical. Scientists alleged the two crafts were flying over New Mexico during an electrical storm in June of 1947, with severe lightning. The two craft collided in midair, with one crashing near Corona and the other crashing in western New Mexico at the base of the Luera Mountains. Let me repeat, the Luera Mountains crash site in western New Mexico was in a remote area and not found for two years.

To the best of my knowledge, there were only two crashes in New Mexico in 1947. I don't know of any other one.

—Richard Doty, as told to Jon Stewart on 26 August 2023

As the years rolled on and history's tapestry unfolded, the Roswell Crash Event continued to cast its enigmatic shadow over time. Among those who dared to delve into its depths, Richard Doty emerged as a key figure, armed with notes that held within them a summation of the event as of 2023.

The pages before him were etched with words that sought to unveil the layers of mystery surrounding that fateful period in late June of 1947. In those bygone days, the saga had begun with the discovery of a debris field on the Brazel ranch: metallic fragments, small yet otherworldly, scattered across the land, igniting curiosity, and setting a chain of events into motion. It was Brazel who collected these pieces of the puzzle and initiated the contact that would reverberate through history—he reached out to the U.S. Army stationed at Roswell Army Airfield.

Yet, as Doty's notes revealed, the Brazel ranch was just one facet of a multifaceted tale. In the annals of that same era, an archaeological team from the University of New Mexico embarked on a journey that would lead them to a crashed aircraft, a vessel not of this world. Within its confines lay an astonishing discovery—an eerie tableau of four lifeless alien bodies and one being that still clung to life. The archeologist's discovery set in motion a series of notifications that would ripple through local law enforcement, eventually reaching the ears of the U.S. Military.

In the intricate dance of secrecy and intrigue, the live alien was transported, as if a relic of an era beyond comprehension, to Kirkland Field, and from there to the clandestine confines of Los Alamos—a place known for its secrets, a crucible of knowledge that had borne witness to the birth of the atomic age.

Doty's notes then transported readers to a different corner of New Mexico, to the vast expanse of Catron County. Here, a rancher tending to his cattle stumbled upon a crash site, a place where the boundaries between the known and the unfathomable were shattered. The account, spanning a tapestry of days and weeks, recounted how the rancher's discovery set into motion a sequence of events that eventually led to the recovery of another crash site and five more bodies.

As Doty's words flowed across the pages, the pieces of this intricate puzzle began to fit together. The two crafts, identical in form, had traversed the skies above New Mexico during a tempestuous electrical storm. Lightning, fierce and wild, had intersected their paths, colliding with the crafts in midair. One craft met its end near Corona, while the other plummeted to the remote reaches of western New Mexico, where it lay undiscovered for two years, a testament to the vastness of the desert's secrets.

In the journey to uncover the truth, Doty's notes stood as a beacon, guiding readers through the labyrinth of history. His words spoke of the convergence of circumstances, the echoes of events that had woven the tale of the Roswell Crash. As he closed the chapter, one message stood clear—a resounding affirmation that, to the best of his knowledge, there existed only two crashes in New Mexico in 1947. A stark testament that, despite the speculative whispers of time, Doty had no knowledge of any other incidents beyond those pivotal moments that had shaped the course of history and shrouded the Roswell Crash Event in a cloak of mystery that continued to endure.

Amidst the currents of history, Richard Doty's revelations in 2023 cast new light upon the Roswell Crash Event. His notes, a tapestry woven with threads of truth, unfolded a fresh summation of the enigma that had captivated minds for decades.

These pages, marked by ink and memory, beckoned readers to journey back to late June of 1947, a time when the world teetered on the edge of the unknown. The story, as recounted in Doty's notes, began on the vast expanse of the Brazel ranch. It was Brazel's initiative that set in motion a sequence of events that would reverberate through history—culminating in a call that would eventually lead to revelation.

No one ever really 'learns' from history, because choices never present themselves in exactly the same way, and because you can always choose similarities and differences to fit current needs.

—James Fallows

Chapter 14

Resonating Encounters—Uniting Witness Perspectives

As the narrative unraveled further, a striking pattern emerged from the witness accounts, painting a hauntingly coherent picture of a second Roswell crash that had remained obscured by time's heavy curtain. This chapter delves into the remarkable parallels among these stories, revealing the astonishing similarities that spanned disparate experiences.

Among those who lent their voices to history were archeologists, immersed in the pursuit of understanding the remnants of the past. Their path led them to the mysterious aftermath of a cosmic encounter, where they stood in awe before an unearthly spectacle. Ranchers, too, entered the tale—a thread that wove through the chapters of time. It was their eyes that first glimpsed the unfolding drama, the enigmatic journey of a glowing fireball hurtling through the heavens.

Lightning storms, those primordial displays of nature's power, took center stage in these stories. They were the backdrop against which destiny played out, two worlds colliding amid the fury of electric tempests. And amid the celestial clashes, three crafts emerged as actors in this cosmic drama—vessels that traversed the gulf between the stars, only to meet their end amidst the chaos of our world.

The descriptions coalesced into a singular image, as if plucked from the dreams of science fiction. Small bodies, each standing no taller than four feet, entered the narrative. The unanimity in their descriptions, their similarity across diverse accounts, lent credence to a truth that could no longer be ignored. These beings were not of our world, yet they found themselves within its grasp. Their attire, a vision of strangeness, was rendered in unison—tight-fitting suits adorned with a helmet-like device, an emblem of their foreign origins.

Ranchers, the unsung explorers of their own lands, stumbled upon these crash sites, unsuspecting witnesses to the momentous events unfolding before them. Their accounts echoed with wonder and disbelief, a testimony to the inexplicable encounters etched in their memories. And then came the soldiers, the agents of the government, sealing off the landscapes as if drawing a veil over the very heart of mystery. A chapter closed, the stories silenced, the echoes of that time whispered only among the shadows.

In a stunning revelation, the landscape itself emerged as a critical character. The undeniable truth settled like a stone—without a doubt, the second crash had unfolded within the confines of the San Agustin Plains, encircled by the sentinels of Horse Peak and the base of the Luera Mountains. This geographical boundary, etched in history, bore witness to the enigma that unfolded within its embrace, a mysterious secret guarded by time itself.

As the threads of these accounts wove together, they formed a tapestry of truth, a revelation that spanned the years to illuminate a reality once obscured. In this chapter, the echoes of witness stories melded into a symphony of certainty, an undeniable narrative that shattered the walls of skepticism. The story of the second Roswell crash was no longer a mere whisper—it had emerged as a resounding truth, a cornerstone of history unveiled.

Compare Scripture with Scripture. False doctrines, like false witnesses, agree not among themselves.

—William Gurnall

Chapter 15

Threads of Corroboration—Recognizing Shared Features

Amidst the intricate details of the witness accounts, a symphony of similarities emerges, painting a portrait of the extraordinary events that unfolded around Roswell. These shared elements, like notes harmonizing in a cosmic composition, bridge the gaps between individual stories, beckoning us to recognize the undeniable connections that underlie the enigma.

The crafts that graced Roswell's skies, though described through varied perspectives, shared a common thread of appearance—a striking yet darker silver sheen that shimmered in the sun's embrace. This consistency in the craft's visual allure speaks to a uniformity that defies coincidence, hinting at an origin far beyond our terrestrial realm.

The beings, central to these chronicles, stood resolute at four feet tall—a convergence that cannot be dismissed as mere chance. As if drawn from the same enigmatic palette, their stature emerges as a signature of cosmic visitors who traversed unfathomable distances to arrive on our doorstep. Some accounts bring forth a curious detail—a headset or helmet that adorned their forms. This subtle yet resonating similarity underscores the

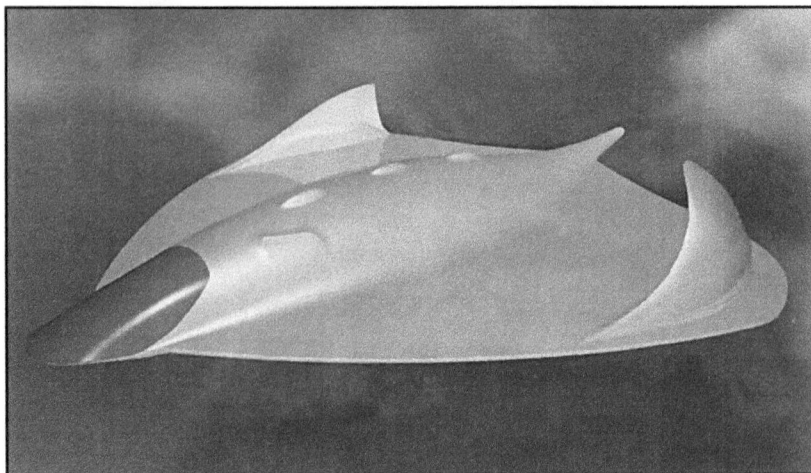

**A rendering of one of the crafts that crashed
outside Magdalena, NM.**

precision with which these accounts have been woven.

A tale of survival takes center stage in the narratives of Dr. Steven Greer and Richard Doty. Their direct testimonies from military personnel paint a vivid picture—one of an alien entity that defied the odds, surviving an encounter that many of its counterparts did not. The emphasis on this lone survivor echoes through the years, etching itself into the story as a testament to the resilience of the unknown beings.

As the crafts embarked on their final journey, a common trajectory emerged—they soared away from the Roswell Army Air Field, tracing their path towards a destination that looms inextricably in the lore—Wright-Patterson. This singular convergence leaves us pondering the mysteries that these facilities might have housed, their secrets perhaps eternally shrouded in the annals of classified history.

The crash sites themselves bear witness to a shared fate—all of the crafts met destruction of varying degrees, their fractured forms mirroring each other in a grim reflection. The unifying presence of deceased occupants in all but the Brazel debris field accentuates the gravity of the events. The consistent observation that these encounters felt akin to a dream for those who experienced them hints at a reality that transcends the ordinary, a realm where the extraordinary takes shape.

As we peer through the lens of time, another parallel comes into focus—the rigidity and, at times, hostility of the military personnel dispatched to guard these crash sites. Their reactions underscore a narrative of secrecy, urgency, and a determination to shield the truth from prying eyes. The confrontations that unfolded at these sites evoke a sense of tension, revealing a hidden struggle between the quest for disclosure and the commitment to containment.

The symphony of shared elements resonates—a silver sheen adorning crafts that defied gravity, beings of four feet of stature that bridged galaxies, tales of survival and destinations of intrigue, shattered forms, survivors, dreamlike encounters, and the clash between the curious and the clandestine. We find ourselves confronted with a truth that transcends the boundaries of individual perspectives, urging us to question the cosmos and our place within it. As we step back from the mosaic of similarity, we are left with a realization that the enigma of Roswell stretches far beyond a singular incident—it is a cosmic melody composed of shared experiences and hidden truths, waiting for those with the courage to listen and the curiosity to unravel.

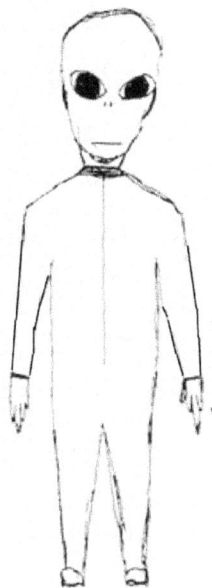

Gerald Anderson's drawing of the alien he saw as a child.

Here is a compilation of similarities of the second crash site:

- Two to three craft in the air
- Crash of an otherworldly metallic object lying on the desert floor
- A group of archeologists students and an archeology professor(s)
- Lightweight metallic shiny material scattered on the ground
- Corporeal beings, 3-1/2 to 4 feet tall
- Humanoid-looking beings, larger heads than humans, spindly arms and legs
- Badly damaged craft and bodies
- Government cordons off area and covers up the crash
- A feeling of dread, surrealism and wonderment by observers
- All accounts have a time frame between late June to early July, 1947
- Five beings, four of them dead, found at the crash site
- One survivor from the crash site dies in 1952
- Craft described as dark matted sterling silver
- E.T. craft brought down via an electric disturbance (new weapon or lightning storm)

I am not one to rely upon the expert procedure. It is the psychology I seek, not the fingerprint or the cigarette ash.

—Agatha Christie's Hercule Poirot

Chapter 16

The Denouement of the Second Roswell Crash

Taking into account the testimony of seemingly ordinary people, we find ourselves constantly circling back to Richard Doty. We must emphasize, as credible investigators, the credibility of Richard Doty's testimony regarding UFO-related occurrences and projects. The authors assert that Doty's background as a former counterintelligence officer is crucial because individuals in such roles typically receive briefings on sensitive matters. This suggests that Doty would have had direct access to classified information related to UFOs. This angle of his credibility adds weight to his claims about these occurrences.

We would also like to highlight Doty's psychological disposition. Doty appears genuinely disgusted with individuals in the UFO community who refute his knowledge. This emotional response could be seen as an indicator of his sincerity, as he had direct access to this information through official briefings. This could be interpreted as his frustration with those who deny his knowledge despite his insider status.

Furthermore, let us not discount Dr. Steven Greer's role in corroborating a significant portion of Doty's testimony. Greer's acceptance among a multitude of former military personnel who have come forward as whistleblowers is noted as unparalleled in history. This endorsement from Greer lends credibility to Doty's claims and places him at the forefront of discussions about the Second Roswell Crash, suggesting that his testimony is particularly significant.

Chapter 17

Some Recent Invaluable Information

During the final stages of preparing this book for publication, we encountered critical information that necessitated immediate inclusion. Consequently, this chapter incorporates a few last-minute additions aimed at ensuring the accuracy and relevance of the content. We understand that this may introduce some discontinuity, but we believe it's crucial to offer you the most current and comprehensive information available.

Astrophysicist & Pentagon consultant Dr. Eric W. Davis

In the context of this book, we'll delve into the work of Dr. Eric W. Davis, PhD, an astrophysicist who has served as a subcontractor and consultant for the Pentagon's UFO program since 2007. Dr. Davis is the Chief Science Officer of EarthTech International, Inc. and the Institute for Advanced Studies at Austin. Dr. Davis's research specializations include breakthrough propulsion physics for interstellar flight, interstellar flight science, beamed energy propulsion, advanced space nuclear power and propulsion, directed energy weapons, future and transformational technology, general relativity theory, quantum field theory, quantum gravity theories, experimental quantum optics, and SETI-xenoarchaeology.

Eric has spent decades working with Robert Bigelow and his paranormal investigation efforts, including the National Institute for Discovery Sciences, and Bigelow Aerospace and Bigelow Aerospace Advanced Space Studies (BAASS). The company he works for now, EarthTech International Inc., is working with the To the Star Academy to analyze anomalous materials.

Dr. Davis's credentials have been authenticated by UFO phenomenon expert Leslie Kean, a respected author and contributor to *The New York Times*. Mrs. Kean has verified to this author that Eric Davis was employed by an Aerospace Corporation and a defense contractor. Furthermore, Dr. Davis stated that he conducted a classified briefing for a Defense Department agency, which included information about retrievals from "off-world vehicles not made on this earth."

What's pertinent to this book is Dr. Davis's public assertion that he had access to a Department of Defense report concerning the Roswell incident. According to Dr. Davis, the report contains information about ten Velobind volumes stored at Wright-Patterson Air Force Base (the former Wright Field), detailing data related to "two crashed Manta-Ray shaped craft, recovered bodies, foil-type materials, and a special study conducted by TRW."

It is important to know especially in regard to Richard Doty, Richard French, and Eric Davis that the restrictions surrounding discussions of classified programs and the ambiguous nature of the information presented in unclassified slides from the briefings have placed officials who have studied UFOs in the position of expressing their views without providing concrete evidence.

Jon Stewart

86

Once you eliminate the impossible, whatever remains, no matter how improbable, must be the truth.

—Arthur Conan Doyle

Chapter 18

Final Chapter: A Perpetual Mystery— Embracing Magdalena's Legacy

As the last pages of the Roswell book turn, a sense of revelation and mystery intertwines, leaving us with a profound understanding that the journey through the enigma of the Roswell incidents is far from over. The quest to unravel the truth within the folds of history has led us through a labyrinth of witness accounts, government secrecy, and unexplained phenomena. Yet even as we draw conclusions, the allure of the unknown lingers, tugging at the corners of our understanding.

The tapestry woven by witness stories has provided us with glimpses into a realm beyond our understanding. Archeologists, ranchers, soldiers, and the echoes of time have come together to craft a narrative that defies explanation. We find ourselves grappling with inexplicable occurrences, tales of strange crafts, unearthly beings, and the residue of cosmic encounters etched upon the landscape.

The convergence of similarities among witness accounts has carved

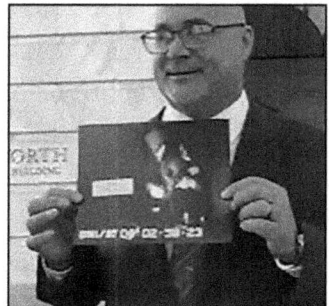

Author Jon Stewart at the nation's capital.

a path toward a truth that refuses to be ignored. The undeniable parallels—glowing fireballs, lightning storms, otherworldly bodies—create a mosaic of veracity. These tales, though diverse in origin, are united by the threads of experience, woven together with an unwavering certainty that cannot be overlooked.

And yet, even in our conclusions, the allure of the unknown whispers to us. As we close this chapter of investigation, we are left with questions that reach beyond the confines of these pages. What lies beyond the boundaries of disclosure?

What truths remain hidden beneath layers of secrecy?

The very essence of these inquiries ignites a yearning within us—a yearning to pierce through the shadows and uncover the enigma that persists.

In the heart of the San Agustin Plains, Horse Peak, and the top of the Luera Mountains, a truth pulses—two crashes, two mysteries, eternally bound to a landscape that holds secrets beyond our grasp. As the final chapter draws to a close, it is our hope that the fire of curiosity continues to burn bright, leading us to delve further, explore deeper, and seek the truths that have eluded us.

The journey undertaken within these pages is but a fragment of the larger narrative that still unfolds. As we part ways with the accounts, the questions, and the mysteries that have held us captive, we step into a world where the unexplained and the extraordinary beckon. The veil of the unknown shrouds our path, enticing us to continue our exploration, to continue seeking, and to continue unraveling the tapestry of the Roswell incidents— one thread at a time.

And so, dear reader, as we conclude this chapter of the events in New Mexico, we leave you with a spark, a spark of curiosity that we hope will ignite your own journey. The enigma of Roswell is not confined to the pages of this book: it is, as Winston

Churchill wrote of the former Soviet Union, "A riddle wrapped in a mystery inside an enigma."

Indeed it is a living mystery, waiting to be unearthed, waiting for your inquiry, your investigation, and your own pursuit of the truth that resides within the shadows. The story continues, the journey persists, and the call of the unknown resonates within each of us, urging us to venture further and uncover the secrets that time has concealed.

I bid you peace. . . .

Jon Stewart
November 28, 2023

List of Images and Photographs

Also available from Pisgah Press & ArsPoetica

POETRY COLLECTIONS

Talking with Ghosts	Victoria Bender
Letting Go	Donna Lisle Burton
Way Past Time for Reflecting	Donna Lisle Burton
From Roots . . . to Wings	Donna Lisle Burton
This Virgin Page	Jim Carillon
Centered	Jim Carillon
And to See Takes Time	Mamie Davis Hilliard
Lessons Learned	Jay Jacoby
Barricaded Bards: Poems from the Pandemic	The Poets of OLLI
With These Hands	Nelson Sartoris
On Wings of Words	Nelson Sartoris
Brain Slivers	Nelson Sartoris
Unsent Postcards	Nelson Sartoris
Invasive Procedures: Earthquakes, Calamities, & poems from the midst of life	Nan Socolow

FICTION

Mombie: The Zombie Mom	Barry Burgess
Gabriel's Songbook	Michael Amos Cody

FINALIST, FEATHERED QUILL BOOK AWARD, FICTION, 2022

A Twilight Reel	Michael Amos Cody

GOLD MEDAL, FEATHERED QUILL BOOK AWARD, SHORT STORIES, 2022

Trang Sen: A Novel of Vietnam	Sarah-Ann Smith

MYSTERY

The Bob & Marcus Mysteries:	H. N. Hirsch

Shade; Fault Line; Rain (coming in 2024)

The Last of the Swindlers	Peter Loewer
The Rick Ryder Mysteries:	RF Wilson

Deadly Dancing, Killer Weed, The Pot Professor, Murder on the Rocks (coming in 2024)

NON-FICTION

Letters of the Lost Children: Japan—World War II	Ron Ferster & Jan Atchley Bevan
Musical Morphine: Transforming Pain One Note at a Time	Robin Russell Gaiser

FINALIST, USA BOOK AWARDS, 2017

Open for Lunch	Robin Russell Gaiser
Reed's Homophones: A Comprehensive Book of Sound-alike Words	A.D. Reed
Swords in their Hands: George Washington and the Newburgh Conspiracy	Dave Richards

FINALIST, USA BOOK AWARDS, HISTORY, 2014

Order from online booksellers Amazon or B&N, or from:

Pisgah Press, LLC
PO Box 9663, Asheville, NC 28815
www.pisgahpress.com

Jon Stewart